Grade 1

Time and Money

Written by Shannon Keeley

Illustrations by Laura Merer

FlashKids

An imprint of Sterling Children's Books

This book belongs to

_____

Published by Sterling Publishing Co., Inc.
387 Park Avenue South, New York, NY 10016
Text and illustrations © 2006 by Flash Kids
Distributed in Canada by Sterling Publishing
c/o Canadian Manda Group, 165 Dufferin Street
Toronto, Ontario, Canada M6K 3H6
Distributed in the United Kingdom by GMC Distribution Services
Castle Place, 166 High Street, Lewes, East Sussex, England BN7 1XU
Distributed in Australia by Capricorn Link (Australia) Pty. Ltd.
P.O. Box 704, Windsor, NSW 2756, Australia

Sterling ISBN 978-1-4114-3450-9

Manufactured in China

Lot #:
16
04/16

For information about custom editions, special sales, premium and
corporate purchases, please contact Sterling Special Sales
Department at 800-805-5489 or specialsales@sterlingpublishing.com.

Cover design and production by Mada Design, Inc.

Dear Parent,

Learning to tell time and count money are important steps in your child's educational development. This book will help your child learn the basics of reading the hands on clocks and identifying and adding coins. Follow these simple steps to make the most of this workbook:

- Find a comfortable place where you and your child can work quietly together.
- Encourage your child to go at his or her own pace.
- Help your child with the problems if he or she needs it.
- Offer lots of praise and support.
- Let your child reward his or her work with the included stickers.
- Most of all, remember that learning should be fun! Take time to laugh at the funny characters, and enjoy this special time spent together.

Classroom Clock

Write the number to which each hand points. Then write the time.

The hour hand points to 8.
The minute hand points to 12.
The minute hand points to 12 at
the beginning of an hour. The
clock on the right shows 8:00.

1.   Hour ↑   Minute ↑

_____   _____   _____ : _____

2.   Hour ↑   Minute ↑

_____   _____   _____ : _____

3.   Hour ↑   Minute ↑

_____   _____   _____ : _____

4.   Hour ↑   Minute ↑

_____   _____   _____ : _____

5.   Hour ↑   Minute ↑

_____   _____   _____ : _____

6.   Hour ↑   Minute ↑

_____   _____   _____ : _____

Chalk O'clock

When the minute hand is on the 12, we say "o'clock." Write the time using "o'clock."

1.  It's __4__ o'clock.

2.  It's ___ __, _____.

3.  It's ___ __, _____.

4.  It's ___ __, _____.

5.  It's ___ __, _____.

6.  It's ___ __, _____.

Time to Match!

Draw a line to match each clock with the correct time.

1. 4 o'clock

2. 8 o'clock

3. 11 o'clock

4. 1 o'clock

5. 2 o'clock

6. 10 o'clock

Race Time

Read the hands on each clock and find the time
on the race path. Mark off each time on the tracks as you go
to find out who gets to the finish line first.

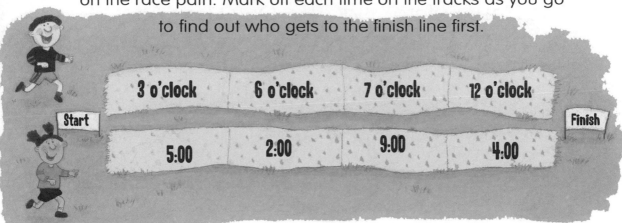

Start   3 o'clock   6 o'clock   7 o'clock   12 o'clock   Finish

5:00   2:00   9:00   4:00

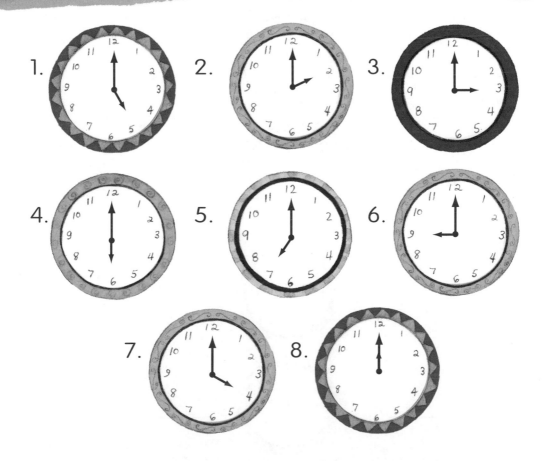

1.

2.

3.

4.

5.

6.

7.

8.

Before and After

Read each clock and write the times for before and after.

One Hour Before · One Hour After

1. _____  _____

2. _____  _____

3. _____  _____

4. _____  _____

5. _____  _____

6. _____  _____

School Schedule

Read the clocks and fill in the chart below.

Reading   —

Math   —

Lunch  —

Science  —

Reading ____:____ ____ — ____:____ ____

Math ____:____ ____ — ____:____ ____

Lunch ____:____ ____ — ____:____ ____

Science ____:____ ____ — ____:____ ____

Full Hands!

Draw the hands on each clock.

1.  3:00

2.  11:00

3.  1:00

4.  5:00

5.  7:00

6.  12:00

Helping Hands

Draw the hands for each time.

Find the time at the bottom of the page and write the letter.

1. 3:00 — S

2. 11:00 — H

3. 5:00 — N

4. 12:00 — D

5. 9:00 — O

6. 4:00 — A

7. 2:00 — E

8. 10:00 — M

‾‾‾‾ ‾‾‾‾ ‾‾‾‾ ‾‾‾‾ ‾‾‾‾ ‾‾‾‾ ‾‾‾‾ ‾‾‾‾
11:00 4:00 5:00 12:00 3:00 9:00 10:00 2:00

Hour Power

Draw the hands and write the time on each clock.

Start

1.  _ _ : _ _ _

2. 2 hours later  ___ : ___ ___

3. 1 hour later  ___ : ___ ___

4. 4 hours later 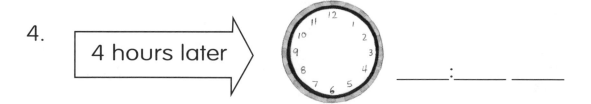 ___ : ___ ___

5. 3 hours later 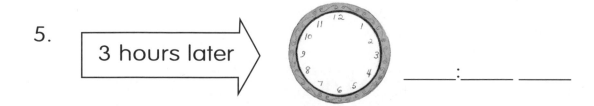 ___ : ___ ___

Library Time

Read the sentences.

Draw the clock hands or write the time to answer each question.

1. The class went to the school library at 11:00. They spent 2 hours there. What time did they leave the library?

2. Sara's class went to the library at 12:00. Ben's class went there 3 hours earlier. What time did Ben's class go to the library?

3. The class left the library at 2:00. They had been there for 1 hour. What time did they arrive at the library? _____:_____ _____

4. The school library opens at 8:00. It closes 7 hours later. What time does the school library close?

_____:_____ _____

Half and Half

When the hour hand is between two numbers and the
minute hand is on the 6, the time is to the **half hour.**
Color the clocks whose minute hands point to the half hour.

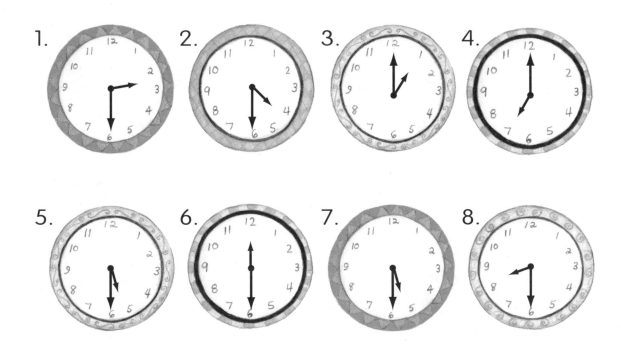

1.

2.

3.

4.

5.

6.

7.

8.

Thirty-Minute Match

When the hour hand is between two numbers, we write the smaller number. When the minute hand is on the half hour, we write 30. This clock shows 3:30 or three-thirty. Read each clock and write the time. Then match each clock with the correct word.

1.  ____:____ ____   ten-thirty

2.  ____:____ ____   seven-thirty

3.  ____:____ ____   four-thirty

4.  ____:____ ____   eleven-thirty

Half-Past Blast

When the minute hand is on the 6, we say it's "half past" the hour.

Read the hands on each clock and write the time as "half past" the hour.

1.

__half__ __past__ __two__

2.

_____ _____ _____

3.

_____ _____ _____

4.

_____ _____ _____

5.

_____ _____ _____

6.

_____ _____ _____

Tic-Tock-Toe

Read the hands on each clock. If the written time matches the clock hands, put an O on the square. If the written time does not match the clock hands, put an X on the square.

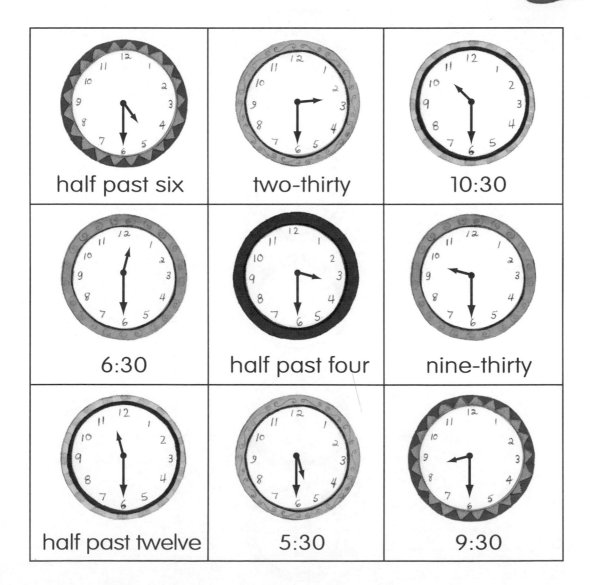

half past six	two-thirty	10:30
6:30	half past four	nine-thirty
half past twelve	5:30	9:30

Before and After

Read each clock and write the times for before and after.

Thirty Minutes Before		Thirty Minutes After
1. _____		_____
2. _____		_____
3. _____		_____
4. _____		_____
5. _____		_____
6. _____		_____

Lend a Hand!

Draw the minute hand on each clock.

1. 12:30

2. 1:30

3. 6:00

4. 4:30

5. 10:30

6. 7:30

7. 6:30

8. 2:00

Play Time!

In this picture, the hour hand is halfway between 8 and 9 to show it is half past eight, or 8:30. Draw the hour hand for each time.

1.

6:30

2.

4:30

3.

12:30

4.

11:30

5.

1:30

6.

9:30

Good Times!

Read the sentences and solve the problems.

1. Jane got to the playground at 12:00. She spent thirty minutes playing on the swings. What time did she finish playing on the swings? _____

2. Chris got to the playground at half past seven. He played until school started at 8:00. How long did he play? _____

3. Justin played on the slide for one hour. He finished playing at 1:30. What time did he start playing? Draw the hands on the clock to show the time.

4. Susan stayed after school to play on the bars. She got to the playground at 2:30. She stayed for an hour and a half. Draw the hands on the clock to show the time she finished playing.

Bus Stop Route

Write the time the school bus
arrives at each bus stop.

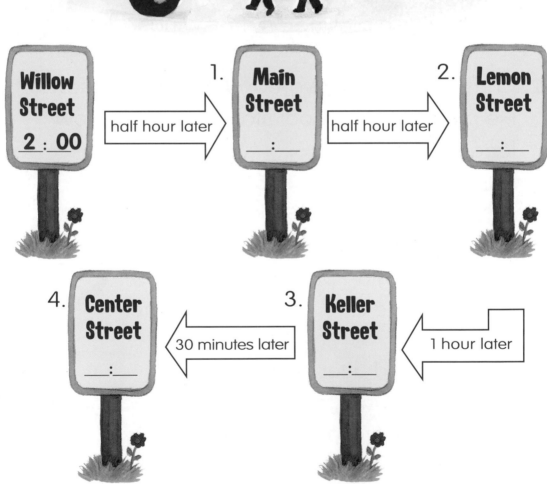

Willow Street

2 : 00

half hour later

1. **Main Street**

___ : ___

half hour later

2. **Lemon Street**

___ : ___

4. **Center Street**

___ : ___

30 minutes later

3. **Keller Street**

___ : ___

1 hour later

Bus Schedule

Look at page 22 to find the time the bus arrives at each stop.
Draw the hands on each clock.

1.
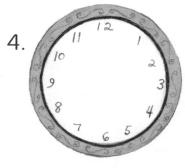

Willow Street

2.
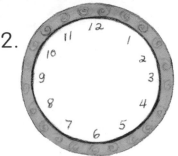

Main Street

3.
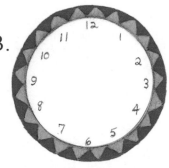

Lemon Street

4.

Keller Street

5.

Center Street

Time to Line Up!

When the minutes hand points to the 3, it is 15 minutes past the hour.

Draw a line to connect each clock with the correct time.

1.    5:15

2.    7:15

3.    11:15

4.    1:15

Minute Maze

When the minute hand points to the 9,
it is 45 minutes past the hour.
To find your way through the maze, connect
the clocks whose minute hands point to the 9.

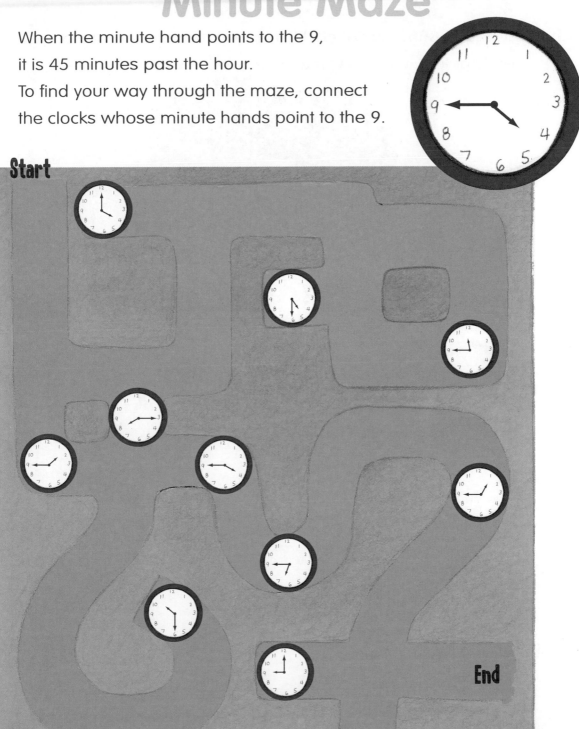

Start

End

Don't Be Late!

School started at 8:15. Look at each clock and decide if the person was early or late. Write the time and circle the correct word.

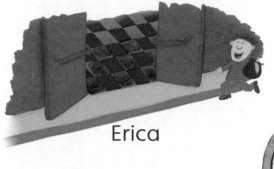

1.  Erica

   _____:_____ _____

   early   late

2.  Dave

   _____:_____ _____

   early   late

3.  Lisa

   _____:_____ _____

   early   late

4.  Brian

   _____:_____ _____

   early   late

Time Flies!

Draw the minute hand for each time.

1.
1:15

2.
6:45

3.
10:15

4.
9:45

True or False

Read each clock and the time below it.
If the time is correct, circle **true**. If not, circle **false**.

1.

4:15
true   false

2.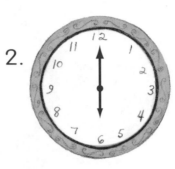

12:30
true   false

3.

3:15
true   false

4.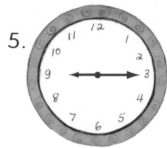

10:00
true   false

5.

9:15
true   false

6.

9:00
true   false

7.

12:15
true   false

Study Buddies

Students are studying for a math test.
Look at the schedule to answer the questions.

Study flash cards . . . . 2:30 – 3:00
Complete workbook pages . . . . 3:00 – 4:00
Do practice test . . . . 4:00 – 4:45
Take break . . . . 4:45 – 5:00
Check test answers . . . . 5:00 – 5:15

1. For how long did they study the flash cards? _____

2. How much time did they have to do the practice test? _____

3. Which activity did they do for 1 hour? _____

4. Which two activities took the same amount of time? _____

It's All in a Day!

Look at each picture. What time does it happen?

Chose a time from the box and write it on the line.

> **12:30 in the afternoon**
> **7:30 in the morning**
> **6:00 at night**
> **2:30 in the afternoon**

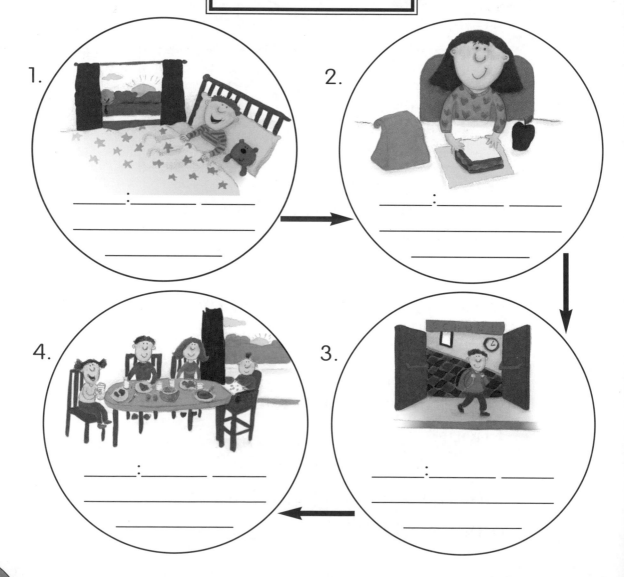

1. ___ : ___ ___
   _____
   _____

2. ___ : ___ ___
   _____
   _____

4. ___ : ___ ___
   _____
   _____

3. ___ : ___ ___
   _____
   _____

When Did It Happen?

Read each activity. Choose the time you think it happened.

1. Breakfast

    7:00 – 7:30

    11:00 – 11:15

2. School

    8:30 – 9:30

    8:00 – 2:30

3. Homework

    8:00 – 5:00

    3:30 – 4:30

4. Dinner

    6:00 – 6:45

    11:00 – 11:30

Minute or Hour?

About how long does each activity take? Circle the answer.

1. sharpen pencil

one minute   one hour

2. take test

one minute   one hour

3. play volleyball

one minute   one hour

4. feed class fish

one minute   one hour

5. drink some water

one minute   one hour

6. do homework

one minute   one hour

Timelines

Draw a line from each picture to the words
that describe how long it takes.

1.

a few hours

2.

about one
minute

3.

several hours

4.

about thirty
minutes

Class Calendar

Look at the calendar to answer the questions below.

OCTOBER

Sunday	Monday	Tuesday	Wednesday	Thursday	Friday	Saturday
1	2	3 book report due	4	5 spelling test	6	7
8	9 science project due	10	11	12 math test	13 field trip	14

1. On what date is the class field trip? _____

2. How many days are in between the spelling test and the math test? _____

3. What is due on October 3? _____

4. What is due on a Monday? _____

5. On what date is the math test? _____

Summer Fun

Look at the calendar to answer the questions.

JULY

Sunday	Monday	Tuesday	Wednesday	Thursday	Friday	Saturday
		1	2	3	4	5
6	7	8	9	10	11	12
13	14	15	16	17	18	19
20	21	22	23	24	25	26
27	28	29	30	31		

1. What day of the week is July 1? _____

2. What is the date for the first Saturday
   in July? _____

3. What date is one week after July 8? _____

4. Independence Day is always on July 4. On what
   day of the week is Independence Day? _____

5. What date is one week before July 20? _____

Penny Poster

Count the pennies in each group. Draw a line to the correct amount.

1.

8¢

2.

2¢

3.

4¢

4.

6¢

One-Cent Wonders

Count the pennies and write the amount.

1.

_____ ¢

2.

_____ ¢

3.

_____ ¢

4.

_____ ¢

5.

_____ ¢

6.

_____ ¢

Five-Cent Fun

Count each group of coins and write the amount.

Then write <, >, or =.

1.

_____ ¢   _____ > _____   _____ ¢

2.

_____ ¢   _____ ¢

3.

_____ ¢   _____ ¢

4.

_____ ¢   _____ ¢

Noah and the Nickel Maze

Help Noah find the way to his piggy bank!

Connect the nickels to find the path through the maze.

Coin Count

Write the amount of each coin.
Add the coins and write the total inside the last box.

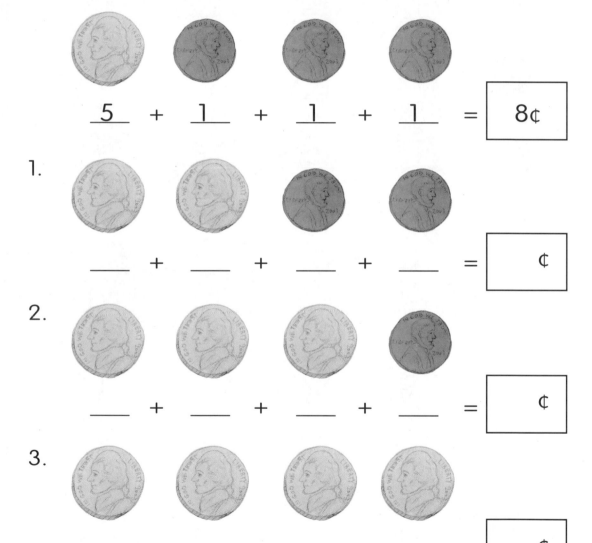

__5__ + __1__ + __1__ + __1__ = | 8¢ |

1.

___ + ___ + ___ + ___ = | ¢ |

2.

___ + ___ + ___ + ___ = | ¢ |

3.

___ + ___ + ___ + ___ = | ¢ |

Mystery Coin

Circle the coin needed to make the amount shown.

amount	needed
1. **12 ¢**	
2. **8 ¢**	
3. **5 ¢**	
4. **21 ¢**	

Pencil Prices

Circle the coins needed to buy each pencil.

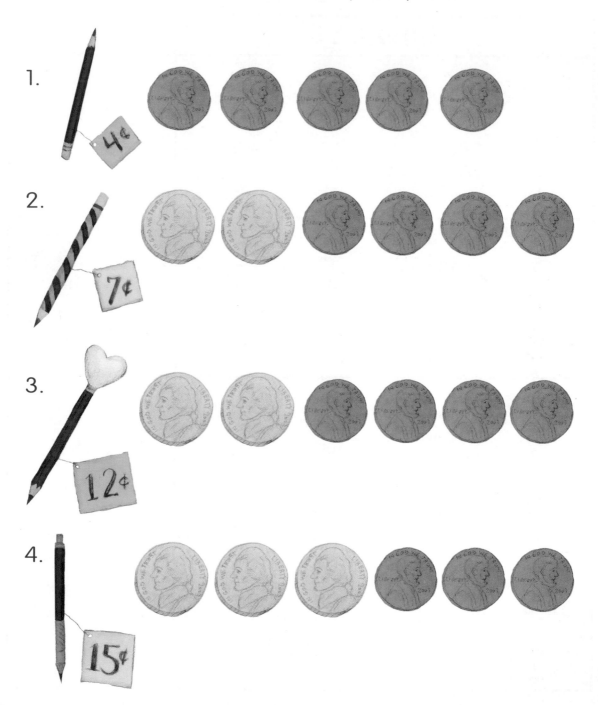

1.

2.

3.

4.

Missing Money

Read the sentences and solve the problems.

1. Sue dropped 3 nickels on her way to school. How much money did she lose?
   She lost _____¢.

2. Rick had 5 pennies. He lost 3 on the playground. How much money does he have left? He has _____¢ left.

3. June had 2 nickels and 2 pennies. She lost 6 cents on the bus. Which coins did he lose?
   She lost _____ and _____.

4. Greg had 4 coins, and he lost them all in the sandbox. He lost 20 cents altogether. What type of coins did he have? He had 4 _____.

Dime Time

Look at each group of coins.
If the coins are equal to a dime, circle **true**.
If not, circle **false**.

1.

   true   false

2.

   true   false

3.

   true   false

4.

   true   false

Dimes in Disguise

Look at each coin. If the coin is not a dime, cross out the letter.

Write the letters in order below to answer the riddle.

1. C

2. D

3. I

4. G

5. M

6. S

7. E

8. T

9. M

10. O

11. N

12. D

What did the coin give to its girlfriend?

A ____ ____ ____ ____ - ____ ____ ____ ____ ring

Desk of Dimes

Count the dimes on each desk and write the amount.

1.
_____¢

2.
_____¢

3.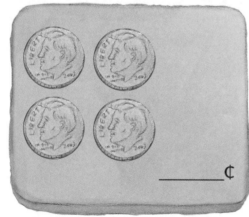
_____¢

4.
_____¢

5.
_____¢

6.
_____¢

Circle It!

Count the coins and circle the correct amount.

1.

11¢   7¢   25¢

2.

17¢   13¢   8¢

3.

3¢   12¢   30¢

4.

25¢   20¢   16¢

5.

40¢   4¢   31¢

6.

15¢   3¢   16¢

Quarter Quiz

Count each group of coins and write the amount.

If the group of coins equals 25¢, write =. If not, write ≠.

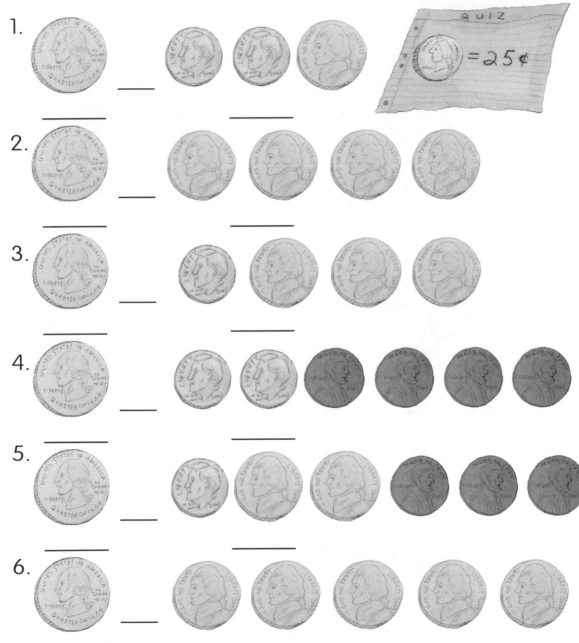

1. ____ ____

2. ____ ____

3. ____ ____

4. ____ ____

5. ____ ____

6. ____ ____

Tic-Tac-Toe

Put an O on all the quarters. Put an X on all the other coins.

Who wins the game?

Quarter Count

Write the amount of each coin.

Add the coins and write the total inside the last box.

1.

    _25_ + _5_ + _10_ = | 40¢ |

2.

    ___ + ___ + ___ + ___ = | ¢ |

3.

    ___ + ___ + ___ + ___ = | ¢ |

4.

    ___ + ___ + ___ = | ¢ |

Classroom Coins

Count how many of each coin are shown in the picture.

Write the number of coins below.

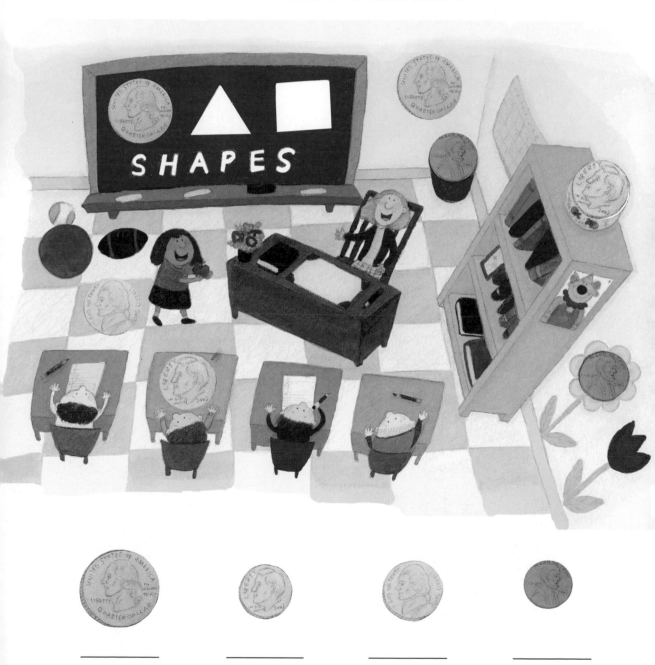

_____   _____   _____   _____

Money Match

Count each group of coins. Draw a line to the coin
that equals the same amount.

1.

A.

2.

B.

3.

C.

Riddle Recess

Read each riddle and answer the question.

1. We are worth 30¢.
   We are all the same coin.
   What are we?
   We are 3 _____.

2. We are worth 25¢.
   We are all the same coin.
   What are we?
   We are 5 _____.

3. We are worth 50¢.
   We are both the same coin.
   What are we?
   We are 2 _____.

4. We are 4 coins worth 22¢.
   We are two different coins.
   What are we?
   We are 2 _____ and 2 _____.

Coins in the Cafeteria

Add the coins for each item. Write the price on the tag.

1.

2.

3.

4.
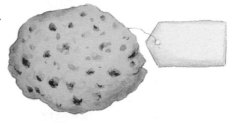

5.

6.
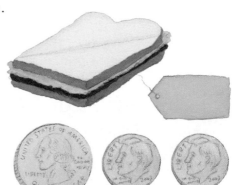

Munch Money

Read about what each child bought for lunch.
Use the prices on page 54. Circle the change.

1. Jane had . She bought .

   Her change was   .

2. Nick had . He bought .

   His change was   .

3. Kate had . She bought .

   Her change was   .

4. Sam had . He bought .

   His change was   .

Coin Race!

Add each group of coins and find the amount on the race path.
Mark off each amount as you go. Who wins the race?

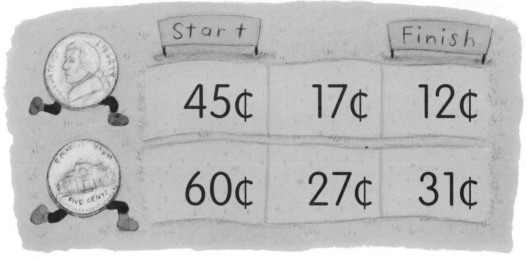

1.

2.

3.

4.

5.

6.

Who Can Buy It?

Add each student's group of coins. Can he or she buy the new notebook?

Circle **yes** or **no**.

37¢

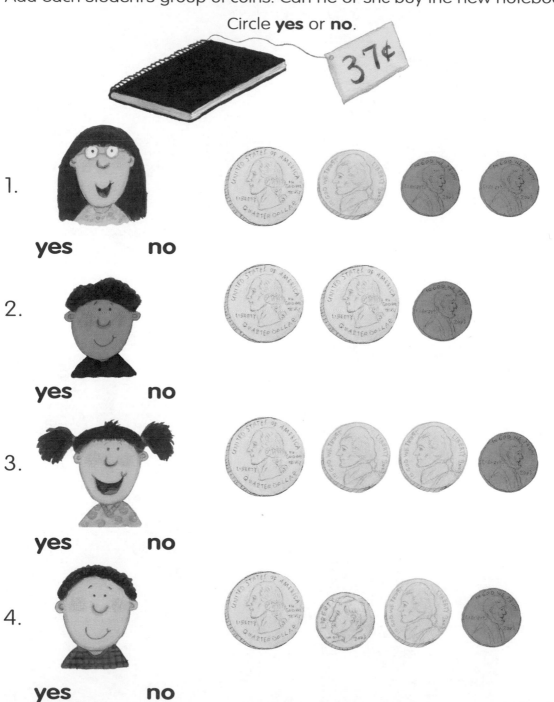

1. yes   no

2. yes   no

3. yes   no

4. yes   no

School Supply Sale!

Circle the coins to match the price of each item.

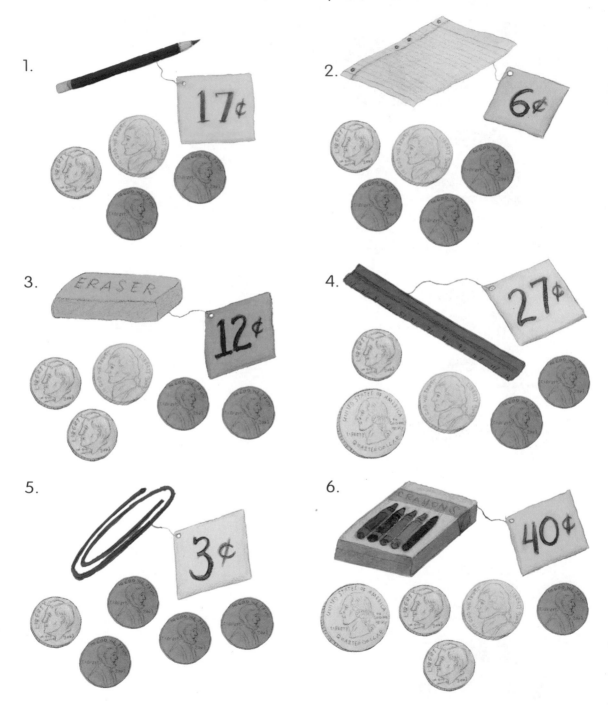

1. 17¢

2. 6¢

3. 12¢

4. 27¢

5. 3¢

6. 40¢

School Spending

Read the sentences. Use the prices on page 58
to answer the questions.

1. Stacey bought  and _____.

   How much did she spend? _____

2. Joan wants _____. She has 3 dimes.

   Can she buy it? _____

3. John had 18¢. He bought 2 items.
   Circle the items he bought.

4. Lori has _____.
   Which item can she buy?

Classroom Cleanup

As the students clean up the room,
some of them find coins!
Read the sentences
and answer the questions.

1.  had . She found a .

How much does she have now? _____ ¢

2.  had . He found .

How much does he have now? _____ ¢

3.  had . She found .

How much does she have now? _____ ¢

4.  had . He found .

How much does he have now? _____ ¢

School's Out!

Read about what Mike did on his way home from school.
Keep track of how much money he has and write the amount.

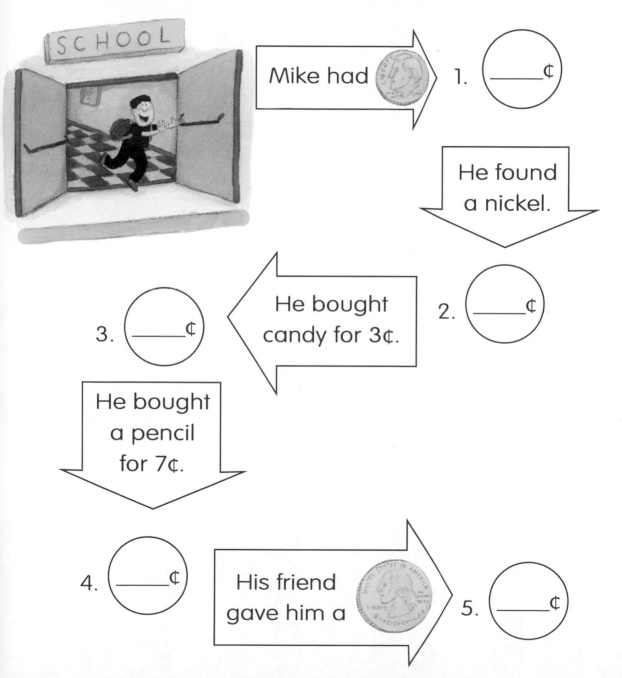

Mike had 🪙

1. (____ ¢)

He found a nickel.

2. (____ ¢)

He bought candy for 3¢.

3. (____ ¢)

He bought a pencil for 7¢.

4. (____ ¢)

His friend gave him a 🪙

5. (____ ¢)

Answer Key

Page 4
1. 3, 12   3:00
2. 6, 12   6:00
3. 1, 12   1:00
4. 11, 12   11:00
5. 9, 12   9:00
6. 2, 12   2:00

Page 5
2. 5 o'clock
3. 12 o'clock
4. 7 o'clock
5. 2 o'clock
6. 6 o'clock

Page 6
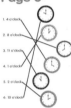
1. 4 o'clock
2. 8 o'clock
3. 11 o'clock
4. 1 o'clock
5. 2 o'clock
6. 10 o'clock

Page 7
1. 5:00
2. 2:00
3. 3 o' clock
4. 6 o'clock
5. 7 o' clock
6. 9:00
7. 4:00
8. 12 o' clock

Page 8
1. 3:00; 5:00
2. 11:00; 1:00
3. 7:00; 9:00
4. 2:00; 4:00
5. 8:00; 10:00
6. 9:00; 11:00

Page 9
Reading 8:00 – 10:00
Math 10:00 – 12:00
Lunch 12:00 – 1:00
Science 1:00 – 3:00

Page 10
1.   2.
3.   4.
5.   6.

Page 11
1.   2.
3.   4.
5.   6.
7.   8.

HANDSOME

Page 12
1. 1:00

2.   3.
   3:00   4:00

4.   5.
   8:00   11:00

Page 13
1.   2.

3. 1:00
4. 3:00

Page 14
1, 2, 5, 6, 7 and 8 should be shaded.

Page 15
1. 4:30; four-thirty
2. 7:30; seven-thirty
3. 11:30; eleven-thirty
4. 10:30; ten-thirty

Page 16
2. half past eleven
3. half past six
4. half past nine
5. half past ten
6. half past four

Page 17
X	O	O
X	X	O
X	O	X

Page 18
1. 10:00; 11:00
2. 2:30; 3:30

3. 4:00; 5:00
4. 6:00; 7:00
5. 11:30; 12:30
6. 9:00; 10:00

Page 19
1.    2.
3.   4.
5.    6.
7. 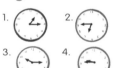   8.

Page 20
1.   2.
3.   4.
5.   6.

Page 21
1. 12:30
2. 30 minutes

3.   4.

Page 22
1. 2:30
2. 3:00
3. 4:00
4. 4:30

Page 23
1.   2.
3.   4.
5.

Page 24
1. 1:15
2. 11:15
3. 7:15
4. 5:15

Page 25

Page 26
1. 8:00; early
2. 8:30; late
3. 9:00; late
4. 7:45; early

Page 27
1.   2.
3.   4.

Page 28
1. True
2. False
3. False
4. True
5. True
6. False
7. False

Page 29
1. 30 minutes
2. 45 minutes
3. Complete workbook pages
4. Take break and check answers

Page 30
1. 7:30 in the morning
2. 12:30 in the afternoon
3. 2:30 in the afternoon
4. 6:00 at night

Page 31
1. 7:00 – 7:30
2. 8:00 – 2:30
3. 3:30 – 4:30
4. 6:00 – 6:45

Answer Key

Page 32
1. one minute
2. one hour
3. one hour
4. one minute
5. one minute
6. one hour

Page 33
1. about one minute
2. several hours
3. a few hours
4. about thirty minutes

Page 34
1. October 13
2. seven days
3. book report
4. science project
5. October 12

Page 35
1. Tuesday
2. July 5
3. July 15
4. Friday
5. July 13

Page 36
1. 4¢
2. 6¢
3. 2¢
4. 8¢

Page 37
1. 5¢
2. 3¢
3. 9¢
4. 7¢
5. 4¢
6. 1¢

Page 38
1. 5 ¢ > 4 ¢
2. 5 ¢ = 5 ¢
3. 5 ¢ < 6 ¢
4. 5 ¢ > 3 ¢

Page 39

Page 40
1. 5, 5, 1, 1   12¢
2. 5, 5, 5, 1   16¢
3. 5, 5, 5, 5   20¢

Page 41
1.   2.
3.   4.

Page 42
1.
2.
3.
4.

Page 43
1. 15¢
2. 2¢
3. a nickel and a penny
4. nickels

Page 44
1. true
2. false
3. true
4. true

Page 45
1. ¢
2. D
3. I
4. ¢
5. M
6. $
7. E
8. 7
9. M
10. O
11. N
12. D
A DIME-MOND ring

Page 46
1. 30¢
2. 50¢
3. 40¢
4. 60¢
5. 80¢
6. 20¢

Page 47
1. 25¢
2. 17¢
3. 12¢
4. 25¢
5. 31¢
6. 16¢

Page 48
1. 25 = 25
2. 25   20
3. 25 = 25
4. 25   24
5. 25   23
6. 25 = 25

Page 49

O	X	X
X	O	X
X	X	O

Page 50
2. 25, 10, 1, 1   37¢
3. 25, 5, 5, 1   36¢
4. 25, 25, 10   60¢

Page 51
Quarters: 2
Dimes: 2
Nickels: 1
Pennies: 3

Page 52
1. B
2. C
3. A

Page 53
1. We are 3 dimes.
2. We are 5 nickels.
3. We are 2 quarters.
4. We are 2 dimes and
   2 pennies.

Page 54
1. 20¢
2. 50¢
3. 35¢
4. 10¢
5. 7¢
6. 45¢

Page 55
1.   2.
3.   4.

Page 56
1. 45¢
2. 60¢
3. 17¢
4. 27¢
5. 31¢
6. 12¢

Page 57
1. no
2. yes
3. no
4. yes

Page 58
1.
2.
3.
4.
5.
6.

Page 59
1. 17¢ + 12¢ = 29¢
2. Yes
3.
4.

Page 60
1. 15¢
2. 40¢
3. 16¢
4. 26¢

Page 61
1. 10¢
2. 15¢
3. 12¢
4. 5¢
5. 30¢

Great work,

_____!

(Name)

You did a super job
learning about
time and money!